Primavera Quick Keys

Primavera P6 Quick Keys

All Contents Copyright © 2015 – myxacom.com.

All rights reserved. No part of this document or the related files may be reproduced or transmitted in any form, by means (electronic, photocopying, recording or otherwise) without prior written permission of the author.

ABOUT THE AUTHOR	3
INTRODUCTION	4
CHAPTER 1 – FILE MENU ASSOCIATED QUICK KEYS	5
CHAPTER 2 - EDIT MENU ASSOCIATED QUICK KEYS	7
CHAPTER 3 - VIEW MENU ASSOCIATED QUICK KEYS	9
CHAPTER 4 – PROJECT MENU ASSOCIATED QUICK KEYS	11
CHAPTER 5 - ENTERPRISE MENU ASSOCIATED QUICK KEYS	12
CHAPTER 6 – TOOLS MENU ASSOCIATED QUICK KEYS	14
CHAPTER 7 – ADMIN MENU ASSOCIATED QUICK KEYS	16
CHAPTER 8 - HELP MENU ASSOCIATED QUICK KEYS	17
PRIMAVERA P6 SHORTCUT KEYS	18
FILE MENU – ALT F	19
EDIT MENU – ALT E	20
VIEW MENU – ALT V	22
PROJECT MENU – ALT P	23
ENTERPRISE MENU – ALT N	24
TOOLS MENU – ALT T	25
ADMIN MENU – ALT A	27
HELP MENU – ALT H	28

About the Author

Michael started his career as a mechanical apprentice in the aerospace industry, since then has worked with some of the largest and most prestigious projects across the world. He has held roles as a scheduler through to consultant engaging with clients and helping them to develop the processes, people and toolsets to implement or improve an organisations project control across projects and programmes.

Michael is a specialist in Earned Value Management, Risk Management and Scheduling and has published numerous articles. His work on Earned Schedule in Europe has been recognised and commended by the inventor of Earned Schedule.

Michael has also presented at numerous international conferences and is considered by his clients to add value in all that is delivered.

Today Michael still consults through his business Xacom Limited and supports a multiple client base utilising a network of associates. More recently myxacom.com has been launched which delivers video tutorials via a membership subscription (visit www.myxacom.com for more details).

More information on Michael and his history, including other publications, can be found on his LinkedIn profile at https://uk.linkedin.com/in/mickhiggins.

Introduction

Primavera P6 is an extremely capable enterprise planning software which is utilised across multiple companies, organisations and markets.

This book contains the quick keys that can be used when running Primavera P6.

This book is for anyone using Primavera P6 or wishing to learn Primavera P6. The quick keys as described in this book are also available as a video tutorial at www.myxacom.com which is a Project Control membership website.

We hope that you find this book useful.

myxacom.com – where knowledge is no weight to carry.

Chapter 1 – File Menu Associated Quick Keys

- To open the File menu in the Primavera P6 menu press Alt and F this will open up the File menu item. There are shortcuts associated with this menu as follows:
    - To create a new project press Alt and F then Shift and N or Ctrl and N when not in the File menu.
    - To open a project press Alt and F then Shift O or Ctrl and O when not in the File Menu.
    - To close all open projects press Alt and F then Shift and W or Ctrl W when not in the File Menu.
    - To go to page setup press Alt and F then Shift and V. Note that Shift and V is also used to print preview, press Shift and V to toggle between both options, select the required one by pressing Enter when it is highlighted.
    - To go to print setup press Alt and F then Shift and S.
    - To go to print preview press Alt and F then Shift and V. Note that Shift and V is also used to access page setup, press Shift and V to toggle between both options, select the required one by pressing Enter when it is highlighted.
    - To print press Alt and F then Shift and P, alternatively if not using thee file menu press Ctrl and P.
    - To import press Alt and F then Shift and I.
    - To export press Alt and F then Shift and E.
    - To send the project press Alt and F then Shift and D.
    - To check in the project press Alt and F then Shift and H.
    - To check out the project press Alt and F the Shift and K.
    - To select the project portfolio press Alt and F then Shift and L.
    - To commit changes to the project press Alt and F then Shift and M or if not using the file menu press F10.

- To refresh the project data press Alt and F then Shift and R or if not in the file menu press F5.
- To see a list of recent projects press Alt and F then Shift and J.
- To exit Primavera P6 press Alt and F then Shift and X.

Chapter 2 - Edit Menu Associated Quick Keys

- To open the Edit menu in the Primavera P6 menu press Alt and E this will open up the Edit menu item. There are shortcuts associated with this menu as follows:
    - To undo a recent action press Ctrl and Z, there is no shortcut key within the edit menu itself.
    - To cut press Alt and E then Shift and T or Ctrl and X if not in the edit menu.
    - To copy press Alt and E then Shift and C or Ctrl and C if not using the edit menu.
    - To paste press Alt and E then Shift and P or Ctrl and V if not using the edit menu.
    - To add press Alt and E then Shift and A or Ins if not using the edit menu.
    - To delete press Alt and E then Shift and L or Del if not using the edit menu. Note that Shift and L is also used to select all, press Shift and L to toggle between both options, select the required one by pressing Enter when it is highlighted.
    - To dissolve an activity press Alt and E then Shift and O.
    - To access the assign sub menu press Alt and E then Shift and I, there is a number of options in this sub menu:
        - Press Shift and R to assign resources.
        - Press Shift and L to assign resources by role.
        - Press Shift and O to assign roles.
        - Press Shift and C to assign activity codes.
        - Press Shift and P to assign predecessors.
        - Press Shift and S to assign successors.
    - To link activities press Alt and E then Shift and K.
    - To fill down data press Alt and E then Shift and W or if not using the edit menu then press Ctrl and E.
    - To select all press Alt and E then Shift and L. Note that Shift and L is also used to delete, press Shift and L to

toggle between both options, select the required one by pressing Enter when it is highlighted. Alternatively if not using the edit menu then press Ctrl and A.
- To open the find function press Alt and E then Shift and F, if not using the edit menu use Ctrl and F.
- To find next press Alt and E then Shift and N or F3 if not using the edit menu.
- To replace press Alt and E then Shift and R, if not using the edit menu then press Ctrl and R.
- To spell check press Alt and E then Shift S or F7 if not using the edit menu.
- To access user preferences press Alt and E then Shift and U.

Chapter 3 - View Menu Associated Quick Keys

- To open the View menu in the Primavera P6 menu press Alt and V this will open up the View menu item. There are shortcuts associated with this menu as follows:
    - For layout press Alt and V then Shift and O.
    - To select show on top press Alt and V then Shift and W.
    - To select show on the bottom press Alt and V then Shift and H. Note that Shift and H is also used for Hint Help, press Shift and L to toggle between both options, select the required one by pressing Enter when it is highlighted.
    - To select time scale press Alt and V then Shift and M.
    - To select filter by press Alt and V then Shift and F.
    - To sort and group by press Alt and V then Shift and G.
    - To access the project spotlight press Alt and V then Shift and P.
    - To access attachments press Alt and V then Shift and T.
    - To see table font and row press Alt and V then Shift and N.
    - To arrange children press Alt and V then Shift and R.
    - To align children press Alt and V then Shift and L.
    - To view the chart box template press Alt and V then Shift and X.
    - To view chart font and colours press Alt and V then Shift and N.
    - To access hint help press Alt and V then Shift and H. Note that Shift and H is also used to select show on the bottom, press Shift and L to toggle between both options, select the required one by pressing Enter when it is highlighted. Alternatively if not using the view menu press Alt and F1.
    - To view the status bar press Alt and V then Shift and S.
    - To zoom press Alt and V and then Shift and Z.
    - To expand all press Alt and V then Shift and E or if not using the view menu press Ctrl + (Using the number keypad).

- To collapse all press Alt and V then Shift and C or if not using the view menu press Ctrl - (Using the number keypad).
- To access and change toolbars press Alt and V then Shift and T.

Chapter 4 – Project Menu Associated Quick Keys

- To open the Project menu in the Primavera P6 menu press Alt and P this will open up the Project menu item. There are shortcuts associated with this menu as follows:
    - To open activities press Alt and P then Shift and A.
    - To open up resource assignments press Alt and P then Shift and S.
    - To open up the WBS press Alt and P then Shift and W.
    - To open up expenses press Alt and P then Shift and E.
    - To open up WP's and Docs press Alt and P then Shift and D.
    - To open up thresholds press Alt and P then Shift and T.
    - To open up issues press Alt and P and then Shift and I.
    - To open up risks press Alt and P then Shift and R.
    - To select default project press Alt and P then Shift and P.

Chapter 5 - Enterprise Menu Associated Quick Keys

- To open the Enterprise menu in the Primavera P6 menu press Alt and N this will open up the Enterprise menu item. There are shortcuts associated with this menu as follows:
    - To open a list of project press Alt and N then Shift and P.
    - To open the enterprise project structure press Alt and N then Shift and E.
    - To open up tacking press Alt and N then Shift and C. Note that Shift and C is also used to access project codes and calendars, press Shift and H to toggle between all three options, select the required one by pressing Enter when it is highlighted.
    - To access project portfolios press Alt and N then Shift and F.
    - To access resources press Alt and N then Shift and R.
    - To access roles press Alf and N then Shift and O. Note that Shift and O is also used to access the OBS, press Shift and O to toggle between both options, select the required one by pressing Enter when it is highlighted.
    - To access the OBS press Alt and N and then Shift and O. Note that Shift and O is also used to access roles, press Shift and O to toggle between both options, select the required one by pressing Enter when it is highlighted.
    - To access resource codes press Alt and N then Shift and S.
    - To access project codes press Alf and N then Shift and J.
    - To access activity codes press Alt and N then Shift and C. Note that Shift and C is also used to access tracking and calendars, press Shift and H to toggle between all three options, select the required one by pressing Enter when it is highlighted.
    - To access calendars press Alt and N the Shift and C. Note that Shift and C is also used to access tracking and activity codes, press Shift and H to toggle between all three

options, select the required one by pressing Enter when it is highlighted.
- To access resource shifts press Alt and N then Shift and E.
- To access the activity step templates press Alt and N the Shift and V.
- To access control accounts press Alt and N then Shift and A.
- To access funding sources press Alt and N then Shift and F.
- To access resource curves press Alt and N then Shift and U.
- To access external applications press Alt and N then Shift and N.

Chapter 6 – Tools Menu Associated Quick Keys

- To open the Tools menu in the Primavera P6 menu press Alt and T this will open up the Tools menu item. There are shortcuts associated with this menu as follows:
    - To schedule the project press Alt and T then Shift and S or if not using the tools menu then press F9.
    - To level resources press Alt and T then Shift and L or if not using the tools menu then press Shift and F9.
    - To apply actuals press Alt and T then Shift and A.
    - To update progress press Alt and T then Shift and U.
    - To access the summarise sub menu press Alt and T then Shift and Z, the menu contains he following items:
        - To summarise open projects press Shift and O.
        - To summarise all projects press Shift and A.
    - To access job services press Alt and T then Shift and J.
    - To store period performance press Alt and T the Shift and O.
    - To disable auto-recognition press Shift and F2.
    - To open up global change press Alt and T then Shift and G.
    - To monitor thresholds press Alt and T then Shift and M.
    - To open up the issue navigator press Alt and T the Shift and I.
    - To access reports press Alt and T then Shift and P, this opens up a sub menu of items. Note that Shift and P is also used to publish, press Shift and P to toggle between the options, select the required one by pressing Enter when it is highlighted.
        - To access reports press Shift and R.
        - To access report groups press Shift and G.
        - To access batch reports press Shift and B.
    - To access the report wizard press Alt and T then Shift and W.

- To publish press Alt and T then Shift and P, this opens up a sub menu of items. Note that Shift and P is also used to access reports, press Shift and P to toggle between the options, select the required one by pressing Enter when it is highlighted.
    - To publish to the project website press Shift and P.
    - To publish activity layouts press Shift and A.
    - To publish tracking layouts press Shift and T.
- To set the language press Alf and T then Shift and N.
- To access the top down estimation function press Alt and T then Shift and E.

Chapter 7 – Admin Menu Associated Quick Keys

- To open the Admin menu in the Primavera P6 menu press Alt and A this will open up the Admin menu item. There are shortcuts associated with this menu as follows:
    - To access users press Alt and A then Shift and U.
    - To access security profiles press Alt and A then Shift and S.
    - To access admin preferences press Alt and A then Shift and P.
    - To access admin categories press Alt and A then Shift and C. Note that Shift and C is also used to access currencies, press Shift and C to toggle between the options, select the required one by pressing Enter when it is highlighted.
    - To access currencies press Alt and A then Shift and C. Note that Shift and C is also used to access admin categories, press Shift and C to toggle between the options, select the required one by pressing Enter when it is highlighted.
    - To access financial periods press Alt and A the Shift and F.

Chapter 8 - Help Menu Associated Quick Keys

- To open the Help menu in the Primavera P6 menu press Alt and H this will open up the Help menu item. There are shortcuts associated with this menu as follows:
    - To access local help press Alt and H the Shift and L. If not using the help menu then an alternative is to press Ctrl and F1.
    - To access information about Primavera press Alt and H the Shift and A.
    - To access the Primavera online help press Alf and H then Shift and O. Alternatively if not using the help menu press Ctrl Alt and F1.

Primavera P6 Shortcut Keys

The following tables summarise the quick keys in Primavera P6. The table columns have ben split into six categories:

Description – Short description of the Primavera P6 function that the Quick Keys will access.

Main Menu Quick Key – Refers to the Quick Key used to access the Primavera P6 main menu items such as File or Edit.

Menu Quick Key – Refers to the Quick Key used to access the function within the main menu area for example New would be accessed under the File main menu.

Sub Menu – In some Menu items there are sub menus such as Report Groups in the Report menu which would be found in the Tools main menu.

Alternative Quick Keys – These are Quick Keys that can be used without running though the menu structure.

Toggle – In some cases there are the same Quick Keys for different functions, where this is the case the Quick Key will toggle between the items.

File Menu – Alt F

Description	Main Menu Quick Key	Menu Quick Key	Sub Menu Quick Key	Alternative Quick Key	Toggle
New	Alt F	Shift N		Ctrl N	
Open	Alt F	Shift O		Ctrl O	
Close All	Alt F	Shift C		Ctrl W	
Page Setup	Alt F	Shift V			Yes
Print Setup	Alt F	Shift S			
Print Preview	Alt F	Shift V			Yes
Print	Alt F	Shift P		Ctrl P	
Import	Alt F	Shift I			
Export	Alt F	Shift E			
Send Project	Alt F	Shift D			
Check In	Alt F	Shift H			
Check Out	Alt F	Shift K			
Select Project Portfolio	Alt F	Shift L			
Commit Changes	Alt F	Shift M		F10	
Refresh Data	Alt F	Shift R		F5	
Recent Projects	Alt F	Shift J			
Exit	Alt F	Shift X			

Edit Menu – Alt E

Description	Main Menu Quick Key	Menu Quick Key	Sub Menu Quick Key	Alternative Quick Key	Toggle
Undo	Alt E			Ctrl Z	
Cut	Alt E	Shift T		Ctrl X	
Copy	Alt E	Shift C		Ctrl C	
Paste	Alt E	Shift P		Ctrl V	
Add	Alt E	Shift A		Ins	
Delete	Alt E	Shift L		Del	Yes
Dissolve	Alt E	Shift O			
Assign	Alt E	Shift I			
Assign Resources	Alt E	Shift I	Shift R		
Assign Resources by Role	Alt E	Shift I	Shift L		
Assign Roles	Alt E	Shift I	Shift O		
Assign Activity Codes	Alt E	Shift I	Shift C		
Assign Predecessors	Alt E	Shift I	Shift P		
Assign Successors	Alt E	Shift I	Shift S		
Link Activities	Alt E	Shift K			
Fill Down	Alt E	Shift W		Ctrl E	
Select All	Alt E	Shift L		Ctrl A	Yes
Find	Alt E	Shift F		Ctrl F	
Find Next	Alt E	Shift N		F3	
Replace	Alt E	Shift R		Ctrl R	
Spell Check	Alt E	Shift S		F7	

User Preferences	Alt E	Shift U			

View Menu – Alt V

Description	Main Menu Quick Key	Menu Quick Key	Sub Menu Quick Key	Alternative Quick Key	Toggle
Layout	Alt V	Shift O			
Show on Top	Alt V	Shift W			
Show on Bottom	Alt V	Shift H			Yes
Time Scale	Alt V	Shift M			
Filter By	Alt V	Shift F			
Group & Sort By	Alt V	Shift G			
Progress Spotlight	Alt V	Shift P			
Attachments	Alt V	Shift T			
Table Font & Row	Alt V	Shift J			
Arrange Children	Alt V	Shift R			
Align Children	Alt V	Shift L			
Chart Box Template	Alt V	Shift X			
Chart Font & Colours	Alt V	Shift N			
Hint Help	Alt V	Shift H		Alt F1	Yes
Status Bar	Alt V	Shift S			
Zoom	Alt V	Shift Z			
Expand All	Alt V	Shift E		Ctrl +	
Collapse All	Alt V	Shift C		Ctrl -	
Toolbars	Alt V	Shift T			

Project Menu – Alt P

Description	Main Menu Quick Key	Menu Quick Key	Sub Menu Quick Key	Alternative Quick Key	Toggle
Activities	Alt P	Shift A			
Resource Assignments	Alt P	Shift S			
WBS	Alt P	Shift W			
Expenses	Alt P	Shift E			
WP's & Docs	Alt P	Shift D			
Thresholds	Alt P	Shift T			
Issues	Alt P	Shift I			
Risks	Alt P	Shift R			
Select default Project	Alt P	Shift P			

Enterprise Menu – Alt N

Description	Main Menu Quick Key	Menu Quick Key	Sub Menu Quick Key	Alternative Quick Key	Toggle
Projects	Alt N	Shift P			
Enterprise Project Structure	Alt N	Shift E			
Tracking	Alt N	Shift C			Yes
Project Portfolios	Alt N	Shift F			
Resources	Alt N	Shift R			Yes
Roles	Alt N	Shift O			Yes
OBS	Alt N	Shift O			Yes
Resource Codes	Alt N	Shift S			
Project Codes	Alt N	Shift J			
Activity Codes	Alt N	Shift C			Yes
Calendars	Alt N	Shift C			Yes
Resource Shifts	Alt N	Shift E			
Activity Step Templates	Alt N	Shift V			
Cost Accounts	Alt N	Shift A			
Funding Sources	Alt N	Shift F			
Resource Curves	Alt N	Shift U			
External Applications	Alt N	Shift N			

Tools Menu – Alt T

Description	Main Menu Quick Key	Menu Quick Key	Sub Menu Quick Key	Alternative Quick Key	Toggle
Schedule	Alt T	Shift S		F9	
Level Resources	Alt T	Shift L		Shift F9	
Apply Actuals	Alt T	Shift A			
Update Progress	Alt T	Shift U			
Summarise	Alt T	Shift Z			
Summarise Open Projects	Alt T	Shift Z	Shift O		
Summarise All Projects	Alt T	Shift Z	Shift A		
Job Services	Alt T	Shit J			
Store Period Performance	Alt T	Shift O			
Disable Auto-Reorganisation	Alt T			Shift F2	
Global Change	Alt T	Shift G			
Monitor Thresholds	Alt T	Shift M			
Issue Navigator	Alt T	Shift I			
Reports	Alt T	Shift P			Yes
Reports	Alt T	Shift P	Shift P		
Report Groups	Alt T	Shift P	Shift G		
Batch	Alt T	Shift P	Shift B		

reports					
Report Wizard	Alt T	Shift W			
Publish	Alt T	Shift P			Yes
Publish to Project Website	Alt T	Shift P	Shift P		
Publish Activity Layouts	Alt T	Shift P	Shift A		
Publish Tracking Layouts	Alt T	Shift P	Shift T		
Set Language	Alt T	Shift N			
Top Down Estimation	Alt T	Shift E			

Admin Menu – Alt A

Description	Main Menu Quick Key	Menu Quick Key	Sub Menu Quick Key	Alternative Quick Key	Toggle
Users	Alt A	Shift U			
Security Profiles	Alt A	Shift S			
Admin Preferences	Alt A	Shift P			
Admin Categories	Alt A	Shift C			Yes
Currencies	Alt A	Shift C			Yes
Financial Periods	Alt A	Shift F			

Help Menu – Alt H

Description	Main Menu Quick Key	Menu Quick Key	Sub Menu Quick Key	Alternative Quick Key	Toggle
Local Help	Alt H	Shift L		Ctrl F1	
About Primavera P6	Alt H	Shift A			
Online Help	Alt H	Shift O		Ctrl Alt F1	

Published by myxacom.com – where knowledge is no weight to carry

www.ingramcontent.com/pod-product-compliance
Lightning Source LLC
Chambersburg PA
CBHW041614180526
45159CB00002BC/858